EM

]

MW00942063

The 7 Things Resilient People Do Differently

(And How They Can Help You Succeed in Business and Life)

Akash Karia

Resilience & Peak Performance Coach

#1 Internationally Bestselling Author of
How Successful People Think Differently

Bestselling Books by Akash Karia

Available on Amazon:

How Successful People Think Differently

How to Deliver a Great TED Talk

How to Design TED-Worthy Presentation Slides

23 Storytelling Techniques from the Best TED Talks

Ready, Set...PROCRASTINATE!: 23 Anti-Procrastination Tools Designed to Help You Stop Putting Things off and Start Getting Things Done

Free Resources

There are hundreds of free articles as well as several eBooks, MP3s and videos on Akash's blog. To get instant access to those, head over to www.AkashKaria.com/Bonus.

RAVE REVIEW FROM READERS

"...**boils complex issues and ideas down to concise actionable material.**"
~ Thomas Lindey

"...**a quick read that can have immediate and long term benefits.** The exercises in chapter two are really good. The advice in chapters 3 and 4 is spot on. I'm going to share it with my three sons."
~ Phil Barth

"Compared to the other self-help books, **this one of the easiest books to follow and implement**, from start to finish."
~ Alnoor Talwar

"**Enlightening, informative, fun!**"
~ Graciela Sholander

"...this book will help you understand your emotions, where they come from, and offer you **practical advice on how to feel better, right away!**"
~ Claudia Svartefoss

"Deceptively simple book...one you'll want to **read over and over with your highlighter.**"
~ Vikki Walton

"...**a great book.** If you're looking to master your emotions and become more resilient, flexible, and ultimately successful..."
~ M. Sean Marshall

"**I'll definitely be reading this book again**, because I spent the whole time analyzing my own thoughts and reactions and found a great deal to work on."
~ Rebecca Vickers

"...**invaluable advice** to help us deal with our emotions..."
~ Daniela Costea

"**...a must for any future leadership training.**"
~ Deepak Lodhia, Author of Emotional Mastery

"**[Akash] has knocked it out of the park**... A great read full of examples...Highly recommended."
~ Jamie Hill

CONTENTS

To my loving parents,
Paresh and Nisha Karia
Because you're the shining examples of resilience...
And love.

"How easily do you bounce back from a disappointment? What is your reaction to change? As an investor, or a board member or an employee, are you seeking stability or impact? Resilience is a skill, one that's probably more valuable than most."

~Seth Godin

define*: resilient

able to withstand or recover quickly from difficult conditions. Example: "babies are generally far more resilient than new parents realize". Synonyms: strong, tough, hardy.

(*via Google)

YOUR FREE GIFTS

As a thank-you for purchasing this book, I'd like to offer you three bonus resources:

1. **Passcode to the Emotional Resilience Quiz**
   Get personalized, individual feedback from our experts on your emotional strengths and areas for improvement. Your results will also pinpoint specific tools in this book to help you achieve greater success in life and business. (Note: Your access code will be given to you later inside the book).

2. **8 Steps to Defeating Any Limiting Label (PDF Guide)**
   Uncover the limiting labels that are putting the brakes on your success.

3. **How to Triple Your Chances of Success (MP3)**
   Discover scientifically backed advice on how to set goals that triple your chances of success.

To get instant access, go here:
www.AkashKaria.com/Bonus

Acknowledgements

This book draws upon the research, teachings and insights of hundreds of academics, philosophers and coaches. While it is difficult to pinpoint any single individual due to the universal nature of these principles, this book has been influenced by the works of Alain de Botton, Amy Cuddy, Brian Tracy, Carol Dweck, Daniel Goleman, John Grinder, Milton Erickson, Richard Bandler, Socrates, Stephen Covey, Tony Robbins and Viktor Frankl.

Furthermore, my study of the fields of psychology, neuro-linguistic programming and peak performance coaching has lent substantially to this book. To all the individuals whose work lays the foundation for these fields, I owe a huge debt.

Images

All images courtesy of Pixabay.com

WE'VE ALL BEEN THERE

~

We've all been there: something that we perceive as negative happens at home, at work, or at school. Perhaps your boss awards a new position to an undeserving coworker, or a friend makes an unkind comment that you just can't shake.

Whatever the case may be, your emotional response—anger, hurt, fear—holds more control over you than you would like.

Before you know it, you're canceling social engagements, pulling on sweatpants, stocking up on pints of Ben & Jerry's ice cream, and even subjecting your closest friends and family to shoulder shrugs and one-word answers.

Now obviously, we're all different.

For some people, this scenario is all too familiar, repeating itself at every detected slight. For others, such a reaction is reserved for only the direst circumstances. Regardless of which description hits closer to home, this book is for you.

Don't think of this as a book for the "emotionally broken" because I believe that no one is emotionally broken. If you find yourself consistently in disempowering emotional states like the one described above, it may be because you're simply not using the tools at your disposal to put yourself in a more empowering state.

Alternatively, even if you consider yourself to be emotionally satisfied, this book will show you how to intensify life's joys and experience even greater excitement, passion, and happiness. At the same time, it will prepare you to handle life's inevitable valleys—those downturns we all have at one point or another—and use them to your advantage. It will show you what emotionally resilient people do differently, how they do it and how you can use the same tools to succeed in life and in business.

So, why is it so important for you to gain control over your emotional states?

Many experts believe that emotional resilience is the #1 key to success—not education and not conventional intelligence.

Don't we all know people who are smart and educated, but lack the fulfillment they desire?

And yet less educated, less intelligent people who have mastered the ability to use their emotions rather than being used *by* them often achieve far more.

In fact, resilience even results in better health! Jan Bruce writes in her *Forbes* article:

> "A recent study on the correlation between resilience and key health and productivity measures found that resilience is the foundation of success and possibility, with high levels of resilience significantly correlating with better health status; higher job satisfaction, morale, and productivity; and lower stress."

With all those benefits, why *wouldn't* you want to develop your emotional resilience?

DISCOVER THE TOOLS TO DO MORE, GAIN MORE, ACHIEVE MORE, AND BE MORE!

The 7 habits of emotionally resilient people explored in this book will give you the tools to master your emotions by ensuring your emotions are the passengers in the car rather than the driver.

This book is the result of pain-staking research and studying. It is based on thorough academic research as well as my own experiences and that of my clients (who range from Fortune 1000 executives to government members to students).

My hope is that the chapters of this book will guide you to break any unproductive emotional habits and train you to master your emotions so that you can enjoy a higher quality of life and have more drive, more RESILIENCE, to pursue your goals and dreams.

But first: What does itmean to truly master your emotions?

To start, let's work on defining this concept by discussing what it is *not*. Emotional mastery does not refer to the stifling or denial of emotions. **Additionally, the goal of building emotional strength is not to somehow make every situation in life happy and rosy.** In fact, the human experience is inherently loaded with unavoidable ups and downs.

So let me assure you before we go any further that it is entirely natural to feel negative emotions when life's challenges and disappointments get you down. The ultimate objective of learning to master your emotions is to prevent those negative emotions from acting as a driving force in your life.

I know it's hard to believe sometimes, but you *are* in control of your emotions, and ultimately, this book is about giving you the tools to choose your emotional response.

How is that possible?

MIND THE GAP

It's pretty simple. There's a gap between a stimulus (what happens to us) and our emotional response and subsequent behavior.

Mind The Gap

In this book, I explain that gap in more detail and show you how you can use it to decide for yourself what the best emotional response is in any given situation.

Once you've mastered this skill—controlling your emotions and using them to steer you in the direction you desire—you will be able to do more, gain more, achieve more, and be more!

Emotionally resilient people who are no longer held back by limiting emotions (no matter how tempting) achieve more success in every area of life. **They can handle the vulnerabilities of intimate relationships, the risks and failures of business, and the ups and downs of life.**

So, without further ado, let's dive into the seven things emotionally resilient people do differently...

"Resilience is the virtue that enables people to move through hardship and become better. No one escapes pain, fear and suffering. Yet from pain can come wisdom, from fear can come courage, from suffering can come strength - if we have the virtue of resilience."

~ **Eric Greitens**

via *National Review*

Chapter One

THE FIRST STEP

~

Habit # 1:
Resilient people acknowledge their emotions,
accept responsibility for them, and learn to
interpret the positive intentions of their
emotions...

YOUR EMOTION IS YOUR REALITY...

Before we can jump into the business of reprogramming our emotional responses, we have to be open and willing to learn. In this context, the learning process begins with the honest acknowledgement of every emotion you experience. Whatever it is—fear, jealousy, joy, loneliness—allow yourself to feel it without any attempt to push it away or change it.

Accept that for the moment, the emotion you are feeling is your reality. This gives you the opportunity to take careful inventory of every feeling you encounter and move on to make a positive change.

We'll talk more about how to make that positive change later in this chapter, but for now, let's examine an example of how the acknowledgement of an emotion might look in real life. Imagine that someone has said something hurtful to you. Naturally, your first reaction is to feel hurt. What happens next, however, depends on your past experiences, your personality, and your current situation.

Perhaps you feel ashamed of feeling hurt, so rather than allowing yourself to feel that way, you attempt to cover up the hurt with anger and indignation (in my years of coaching, I've seen many people who do this). After all, admitting that you feel hurt would mean admitting that the offending individual's opinion matters enough to really affect you. Does this situation sound familiar? Do you know someone who reacts this way? Have you ever reacted this way?

If you're working toward emotional resilience, there are a couple of things wrong with the scenario described above. For one, covering up the initial feeling of hurt takes energy and effort that would be better spent improving your outlook. Additionally, when you're attempting to learn from your emotions, it's important that you're analyzing the emotions that you feel as a direct response to stimuli—not the ones that you use to cover up your initial feelings.

Finally, and this is important, don't pass judgment on yourself for the emotions you feel as a natural part of life.

In the example above, the feeling of hurt seems somehow unacceptable, so anger takes over—masking the fact that what you really feel is pain.

Researchers have found that suppressing thoughts and feelings can actuallybackfire. For example, a study published in a 2007 issue of the journal *Behaviour Research and Therapy*recounts an experiment conducted by psychologists Richard Bryant and Fiona Taylor to learn about the impact of thought suppression on dreams. The 100 study participants were instructed to choose an unwanted thought, memory, or image that had in the past invaded their minds. Half of the participants were told to attempt to suppress that negative thought for five minutes before going to sleep. According to entries made in dream journals by the participants, those who were told to suppress unpleasant thoughts were more likely to dream about them in their sleep.

Thought suppression can backfire

Bryant explains that this happens as a result of the brain's "distraction" and "detection" processes; as a result of the brain's effort to distract itself with more pleasant thoughts, it actually places itself on high alert attempting to detect any sign of the original negative thought. He says, "People who are highly anxious, or have a lot of things on their mind, the distraction process suffers, allowing the detection process to predominate, and they are going to think more about the unwanted thoughts." Interestingly, for participants who were not predisposed to suppression, the study found no correlation between thought suppression prior to sleep and dream content.

Only those who already had a tendency to suppress their thoughts experienced the phenomenon described above.

So decide for yourself that from this point forward, your head will be a judgment-free zone. **It's essential that you allow yourself to acknowledge rather than suppress the emotions that come your way so that you can identify them accurately, learn more about them, and eventually even learn to manage them.**

What feelings have you been suppressing?

What is causing those feelings, and what do you need to do to free yourself from them?

WHO IS RESPONSIBLE? (HINT: IT'S YOU)

When it comes to our emotions, we generally tend to play the victim—completely helpless in our position of passivity to make any sort of change for the better.

Here's an example:

On Monday morning, you get cut off by multiple drivers in heavy traffic on your way to work and end up running 20 minutes late. Before the day has even gotten off to a real start, you're feeling frustrated, angry, and rushed, and you resent the traffic, construction crews, and other drivers on the road for making you feel that way.

Is this sounding familiar?

Stuck in a jam?

After all, it's not like you *chose* to feel this way, right?

This is the part where I tell you that you're wrong, and that there's hope! We actually can choose how we feel, but we can't do that until we stop letting others control us and *accept responsibility for our own emotions*. Accept that the only reason you're feeling the way you do is because you've allowed yourself to feel that way.

I know this is a tough concept to grasp, but it is possible to be accountable for your own emotions. When something that someone else has said or done upsets you, it's all too natural to immediately pass blame for your hurt and anger to the offending person. Instead, recognize that we've essentially spent years programming ourselves to react a certain way to certain stimuli based on our preconceived beliefs and priorities.

So stop passing blame and accept responsibility for your emotions, because you *do* have a choice!

WHAT IS THE POSITIVE INTENTION?

Once you've begun accepting responsibility for your emotions, you have a real opportunity to learn from them. They can communicate important information to you and help you understand *why* you are feeling or acting in a certain way. In fact, many experts believe that **every negative emotion is actually accompanied by something called a "positive intention."**

Robert Dilts is an expert in the field of neuro-linguistic programming, which examines the relationship between the mind, the language we use, and the way we behave. Dilts has written extensivelyabout the concept of positive intention, providing examples of how certain negative emotions and behaviors are motivated by something positive. He writes:

> "The positive intention behind 'aggressive' behavior, for example, is often 'protection'. The positive intention or purpose behind 'fear' is usually 'safety'. The positive purpose behind anger can be to 'maintain boundaries'. 'Hatred' may have the positive purpose of 'motivating' a person

to take action. The positive intentions behind something like 'resistance to change' could encompass a range of issues; including the desire to acknowledge, honor or respect the past; the need to protect oneself by staying with the familiar, and the attempt to hold onto the positive things one has had in the past, and so on."

This concept of positive intention is really valuable in a discussion of human emotions and our ability to understand them and change for the better.

Although the expression of a negative emotion may not be ideal, it always comes with a positive intention. **People who are emotionally resilient are able to use this to their advantage by looking for the positive intention behind the negative emotion they're feeling.** They dig deep and discover the signal—the message, or intention—that the emotion is sending them. **Like a detective, resilient people ask, "What is the true purpose of this emotion?"**

Be a detective

It may not always be clear, but subconsciously, our emotions provide some benefit for us. Haven't there been times when, because you were sad, you somehow felt more "connected" to and loved by yourself? Especially if you are the kind of person who is always taking care of others, perhaps you were able to find a measure of love for yourself when you finally broke down and gave into the sadness.

Similarly, anger can often provide a sense of self-worth, providing a burst of energy and preparing you to do something…to take action. It gives you a sense of power.

MY STORY

When my ex-girlfriend cheated on me, I was angry and bitter at first. The temptation was to think that the message was, "Relationships result in hurt," but that was a mistake because it was a premature conclusion without the full exploration of my feelings.

So, digging deeper (which took several weeks), I saw that I had initially mislabeled the emotion; while there was certainly some anger, the true emotion that I uncovered was hurt. I was hurt that I had been cheated on, and deeper still, I was scared that I had been cheated on because I was not worthy enough of love.

The signal of both of these emotions—the hurt and the fear—was that I needed to cultivate a stronger sense of worth. I needed to strengthen my self-esteem to the point where my worth would be tied not to someone else's treatment of me, but to myself. So I began slowly building my self-esteem and self-love so that I could love and be loved without my self-esteem ever being purely a function of someone else's treatment of me.

As you may have guessed, it isn't always easy to investigate negative emotions to uncover their positive intentions. **Even emotionally resilient people may be tempted to stop at a shallow message of anger and bitterness from time to time. The difference is that they keep digging until they find a diamond in the rough**, or a message that gives them the power to move forward positively in life. (It doesn't matter WHAT message you discover—as long as the message you discover is one that keeps you moving forward rather than one that drags you backwards.)

THE MOST POWERFUL EXAMPLE OF EMOTIONAL RESILIENCE

One very powerful example of the power of creating emotional change despite the most grim and difficult circumstances is Viktor Frankl, a prominent Jewish psychiatrist and neurologist living in Vienna in the early 1940s. In September 1942, Frankl was arrested and transported to a Nazi concentration camp. As he entered the camp, they took the last of his belongings—including his clothes, his wedding ring, and the manuscript of a book he was writing.

Auschwitz, a Nazi extermination camp in Poland

Like millions of other Jewish prisoners, Frankl suffered inhumane treatment at the hands of his Nazi guards—from starvation and exhaustion to sickness and unending labor. On top of all this, he later learned that his wife, father, and brother had been killed in other camps.

In his book *Man's Search for Meaning*, Frankl wrote, **"The one thing you can't take away from me is the way I choose to respond to what you do to me. The last of one's freedoms is to choose one's attitude in any given circumstance."** This means choosing joy over sorrow, strength over weakness, or hope over despair. Every living person has a choice, and no behavior is dictated solely by circumstance.

Rather than denying or wallowing in his negative emotions, Frankl acknowledged the pain and suffering he was feeling and then, as difficult as it was, set about searching for the positive intention and purpose of the pain.

Ultimately, he realized the pain was there as a teacher to help him create an inner victory. **He understood that even when we cannot control our external circumstances, we can control our emotional reactions and generate an inner victory**. Exhibit A: after Frankl was released from the camp, he resumed work as a psychiatrist and worked to help *others* find meaning in their pain.

So the first step to become an emotionally resilient person is to understand there is nothing wrong with you; accept that your emotions are your reality. Then, take responsibility for your emotions so you can change them, and understand that every emotion has a positive intent. You can learn to consciously take control of your feelings and turn disempowering emotions into empowering emotions by:

1) Digging down deep and acknowledging the *true* emotion you're feeling; and

2) Uncovering an empowering signal or meaning that allows for positive action. Don't stop uncovering until you find a meaning that empowers, rather than disempowers, you.

IN A NUTSHELL

What Most People Do:

Non-resilient people:

- Hide and suppress their true emotions
- Blame others for how they feel
- Do not look for the positive intentions of their emotions

What Emotionally Resilient People Do Differently:

Resilient people:

- Acknowledge their emotions
- Accept responsibility for their emotions
- Learn to interpret the positive intentions of their emotions

Free Bonus:

Passcode to the Emotional Resilience Quiz

Get personalized, individual feedback from our experts on your emotional strengths and areas for improvement. Your results will also pinpoint specific tools in this book to help you achieve greater success in life and business. Your ACCESS CODE is **7263**. Please redeem it on:

www.AkashKaria.com/Bonus

"Your body language doesn't merely reflect your emotions,
it's often the cause."

~ Christian Jarrett

via *99U*

Chapter Two

A TOOL THAT WORKS WONDERS

~

Habit 2:
Resilient people master their emotions through their physiology

---

When you were growing up, do you remember your mother (much like mine) constantly reminding you to sit up straight, stop slouching, and stop dragging your feet? I sure do.

As it turns out, mom's guidance and admonitions may have been valid in more ways than one. Think about it. When it comes to emotions, your body language tends to reflect the way you're feeling on the inside.

For example, if you're feeling sad, you might droop your shoulders, frown, and look down at the ground. When you're feeling proud or happy, your shoulders and head are both held high.

So what happens when we flip this around?

Can we use this information to change the way we feel?

JUST TWO MINUTES...

There's actually been some tremendous research done by Amy Cuddy, a professor at Harvard University, about the power of body language (www.AkashKaria.com/Amy).

In her research, Amy Cuddy found that when people adopt power postures—that is, when they take up as much space as they need by standing or sitting straight with their shoulders back, chest out, feet planted shoulder-width apart, and breathing deeply from the belly—two things happen. Within just two minutes:

1) **Testosterone levels *increase* by 20%.** Testosterone is the hormone in both men *and* women responsible for confidence. Imagine feeling 20% more confident within just two minutes!

Here are two examples of high-power postures (via Buffer)

2) **Cortisol *decreases* by 25%.** Cortisol is the hormone responsible for stress, so imagine, in addition to feeling 20% more confident, you're also feeling 25% less stressed within just two minutes! Doesn't that sound good?

Amy Cuddy speaking at TED *on the power of body language:*
www.AkashKaria.com/Amy

In fact, Carol Kinsey Goman, a body-language expert, says in her *Forbes* article that good posture makes us tougher:

> "A joint study by the USC Marshall School of Business, and J.L. Rotman School of Management at the University of Toronto, found that by simply adopting more dominant poses (open and expansive posture), people felt in control and were able to tolerate more physical pain and emotional distress."

So let's give this a try. I want you to go ahead and stand.

DO THIS...

Yes, I'm serious. Actually stand up; just reading is not enough. You have to experience this for yourself.

So are you up? Great!

Now stand the way you would if you were feeling depressed. Once you've assumed that posture, let's take a look at what you're doing.

Are you standing up straight? Or hunching over? (Hunched!)

Are your shoulders held back and upright or dropping forwards? (Dropping!)

Is your chest out and up or is it sinking down to the floor? (Sinking!)

Are you breathing deep from your belly, or is your breathing very shallow? (Shallow!)

Congratulations! You now know how to get yourself feeling depressed *any time you want.*

But in all seriousness, how easy do you think it is to snap yourself out of that state?

It can be *very* quick, but only if you choose to make it so!

The moment you change your physiology—let's say you're feeling unhappy because you're focusing on sad memories—you break the emotional pattern of unhappiness. Try being unhappy when you have a *big grin* on your face. Add some jumping up and down and dancing to your favorite song, and suddenly, being unhappy is very difficult to do!

One 1988 study actually found a connection between the act of smiling and participants' sense of humor. Each individual was asked to hold a pen in his or her mouth, but only half of the participants were asked to hold the pen in such a way that activated the muscles used for smiling. When the participants were shown cartoons, the individuals using their smiling muscles to hold the pens rated the cartoons as being funnier when compared to the ratings of those who were not using their smiling muscles.

So smile! Because even if it doesn't feel sincere, this small act can positively impact your outlook.

Finally, in addition to posture and facial expressions, you can use breathing as a tool to alter your emotional state. A study conducted by Pierre Philippot set out to determine whether specific emotional states produce unique respiratory patterns. During the study, participants were asked to produce basic emotions—such as anger, sadness, joy, and fear—by manipulating their breathing. Once the subjects felt as though they had reached the desired emotion, they were asked to fill out a questionnaire that helped them describe their breathing.

The study ultimately found that while some emotions are easier to generate than others through the manipulation of respiratory patterns, the basic emotions included in the study *were*, in fact, associated with specific breathing tendencies. For example, sighing was particularly associated with participants feeling sadness, while joy seemed to result in regular, relaxed breathing—often through the nose. I believe that, just as with body language, this correlation also works in the reverse (in other words, changing your breathing patterns will change how you feel).

As you're working to improve your ability to control your emotions, take some time each day to think about how you feel and how you are breathing. Are you relaxed and breathing regularly and evenly from your belly? If you're feeling angry or afraid, is your breathing uneven, rapid, or shallow?

Let's do one final physical exercise to practice breathing. Starting with your eyes closed, focus on feeling joy. Begin breathing in through your nose from deep in your belly. Keep your breaths steady and even, imagining that your stomach is a balloon that inflates with every breath. If it helps to think about a memory or fantasy that is particularly joyful, feel free to do so!

Keep breathing steadily for a couple of minutes— flooding your brain with oxygen and changing your body's biochemistry to result in a calmer, more peaceful state.

Then, while continuing your relaxed breathing pattern, adjust your posture and facial expression to optimize the experience. Roll your shoulders back, and hold your chin parallel to the ground, even allowing a little bit of a smile to spread across your face.

How are you feeling now?

Hopefully some combination of joyful, relaxed, or peaceful. So next time you are experiencing a negative emotion, remember this exercise, and spend a few minutes concentrating on how you can change your physiology to change your mood.

IN A NUTSHELL

What Most People Do:

Non-resilient people:

- Adopt low-power postures when they're feeling down

What Emotionally Resilient People Do Differently:

Resilient people:

- Change their body language to change how they feel
- Utilize the power of breathing and facial expressions to master their emotional states

"Resilience (or resiliency) is our ability to adapt and bounce back when things don't go as planned. Resilient people don't wallow or dwell on failures; they acknowledge the situation, learn from their mistakes, and then move forward."

~ Mind Tools

Chapter Three

HOW TO ADJUST YOUR FOCUS

~

Habit 3:
Resilient people consciously control meaning through focus

Do you remember when we discussed earlier how we have more or less programmed ourselves to react to certain stimuli (things that happen to us) in certain ways, based on our preconceived beliefs and priorities?

Well, in this chapter, we're going to delve more deeply into this idea. The reason we are programmed to a react a certain way to certain events is because our brain takes these stimuli and attaches meaning to them. This meaning—largely defined by experiences we've had or beliefs we hold—causes us to feel a certain emotion, which then results in a behavior.

If you were to change the meaning you attach to the stimulus, then it's possible that you could produce an entirely different emotion and resulting behavior. You're the one in control here—not other people and not circumstances. The sooner you understand that, the sooner you can begin to take advantage of that control and change your life for the better.

A TALE OF TWO EMPLOYEES

Here's an example: imagine that two people get fired. One person can take that to mean, "My life is over, and I'll never be able to find a job as good as this one again!"

On the other hand, another (more resilient) person may initially feel the same hurt, but then choose to assign a different meaning. This person may say, "This is a blessing in disguise because now I can change career paths, go back to school, or open that restaurant I've always been meaning to!"

I know that when these two options are written down sidebyside, the choice seems very clear. Why would *anyone* want to be that first person?

But in reality, we are often unaware of the meaning we attach to certain situations—we just run on autopilot, assigning the first meaning that comes along rather than making a conscious analysis of which meaning will serve us better in the longrun.

Can you think of an event in your past that triggered you to have a negative emotional response?

Why did you respond the way you did?

What kind of meaning did you attach to the event?

Can you see the correlation between the meaning you assigned and the emotion that resulted?

Try re-imagining the event, but assign a new meaning to it. Now that some time has passed, it might even be easy to interpret the event's meaning in a more positive way. What kind of emotion would result from this more positive meaning?

Is it a more positive emotion than the one you felt originally? How would this have changed your behavior? By becoming more familiar with the links between stimuli, emotions, and behavior, you can increase your awareness of your ability to master your emotional responses.

Now you're not going to master them overnight, and it will definitely take some practice, but by just reading this section, you're off to a good start. **Simply the *awareness* that you have the option to assign a variety of different meanings to any given stimuli will be tremendously helpful in analyzing and shaping your emotions.**

ADJUSTING MEANING BY ADJUSTING FOCUS

While we're on the topic of consciously assigning meaning to events, there's another layer to discuss that plays into your ability to assign a positive meaning to external stimuli. That layer is your focus.

The word "focus" could be used in a couple of different ways, but for the purposes of our discussion, we're going to use "focus" to define where we are directing our attention. Your focus is where your attention goes, and it's very important. **I've learned that as a universal principle, people tend to get more of whatever they have set their focus on.**

So if you focus on how great your life is, you'll begin to notice more great thingsin your life. If you decide to focus on the business opportunities available in your community, you'll begin to see opportunities that you would have missed before. On the other hand, if you focus on what you're lacking in your life, you'll begin to notice a lot more areas of your life where you're lacking.

You can think of your focus as a kind of lens through which you view your life and all of the challenges that it brings. The meaning that you assign to each event will be colored by whatever you have chosen to focus on overall. For example, if you tend to focus on being the best at everything—at work, at school, at play—you may read any challenge or shortfall as meaning that you have failed. Resulting emotions may include disappointment, frustration, anger, jealousy, or other negative emotions. The behavior resulting from your emotions is unlikely to be positive as well.

What lens are you using?

So by shifting your focus to something more positive or productive, you actually make it easier for yourself to assign positive meanings when you encounter less than ideal circumstances.

IN A NUTSHELL

What Most People Do:

Non-resilient people:

- Allow life to direct their focus
- Focus on things that put them into disempowering emotional states

What Emotionally Resilient People Do Differently:

Resilient people:

- Consciously control the meaning of events by directing their focus
- Focus on things that put them into empowering emotional states

"Most people live lives of quiet desperation because they focus on things that they cannot control: outside events, stuff that happened in the past and what other people are thinking. As a result, they fail to focus on what they CAN control: their own beliefs, their own attitude, their own emotions, and their own behavior."

~ Geoffrey James

via *Inc*

Chapter Four

THIS CAN MAKE YOU HAPPY, OR IT CAN MAKE YOU SICK

~

Habit 4:
Resilient people mold their belief system

As we've discussed in previous sections, our beliefs play an important role in shaping the way we respond emotionally to external stimuli because they impact the way we interpret and view those stimuli. For this reason, they are very powerful.

Our beliefs are so powerful, in fact, that they can impact us physically—both curing and causing sickness. **Take the placebo effect, for example; some patients, when given essentially fake or ineffective medications or treatments, begin feeling better simply because they expect that the medication will make them better.**

"I'M SICK...I DON'T WANT TO GO TO SCHOOL!"

Your beliefs can also make you sick.

When I was in high school, I can remember waking up and dreading going to school so much that I could literally think myself sick! When my mother would try to get me out of bed, I'd say, "I'm sick," and pretend that I was when I wasn't. I knew that if my mom caught me lying, I'd be in big trouble, so it had to be convincing. I learned to actually believe my own lies!

I'd believe with such certainty that I actually was sick that soon I would begin to feel a headache, dizziness, and even a fever. The moment my mom went to work, the symptoms were suddenly gone, and on came the TV! I could do the exact same thing again the next day.

So as this example demonstrates, our beliefs can have great power over us. While it is possible to use this to our benefit, **not all of our beliefs are productive.** In fact, we each have certain beliefs that are quite disempowering. For example, some of us might believe, "I will be happy when I'm rich." This belief is disempowering because you are teaching yourself that you need money in order to be happy. Similarly, others may believe, "I will be happy when my body is skinny" (i.e., "I believe happiness is a result of how I look").

Beliefs like these, which put conditions on your desired emotional states (happiness, excitement, fulfillment, joy), by their very definition limit the amount of time you are able to experience that emotion. Thus, you should strive to make the conditions for achieving the desired emotional state as easy as possible:

- *"I will be happy when I am rich!"* becomes *"I am happy because I'm alive!"* In this example, the condition goes from having a certain amount of money to simply being alive.

- *"I will be happy when my body is skinny"* becomes *"I will be happy when I go for a run."* In this example, the condition goes from "being skinny" to the much easier to achieve and control "go for a run."

Similarly, try making the conditions for undesired emotional states as difficult as possible to minimize the number of circumstances resulting in negative emotions such as sadness, anger, disappointment, anxiety, etc.

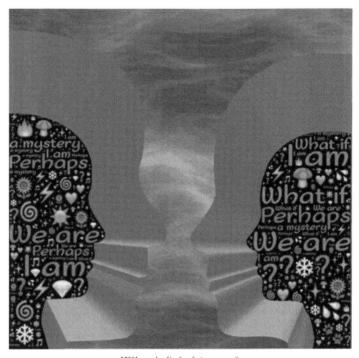

What beliefs drive you?

Other beliefs we have may be based on generalizations we make regarding the world around us. These beliefs can have a very significant impact on our outlook and behavior. For example, what do you think your approach toward life and state of emotion would be if you believed:

- *"Life is a competition, and you're either winning or losing."*

- *"People are naturally selfish, so you cannot rely on anyone else to look out for you."*

You can change your physiology, your language, and your focus, but as long as you harbor those beliefs about life, they're going to play a role in shaping your emotions.

Take a few minutes to answer these three questions by writing down as many things that come to mind:

1. What are your major beliefs about what you need in order to be happy, excited, or fulfilled?

_____

_____

_____

_____

_____

_____

_____

_____

2. What are your beliefs about what needs to happen in order for you to be unhappy, frustrated, or angry?

_____

_____

_____

_____

_____

_____

_____

3. What are your beliefs about the world? Are they empowering or disempowering?

_____

_____

_____

_____

_____

_____

_____

_____

If you discover that you have beliefs that are limiting you, how do you go about changing them? Try following this step-by-step process that I use successfully with my clients:

1. Question your beliefs: are they really true? Under what circumstances are they not true?

_____

_____

_____

_____

_____

_____

_____

_____

2. Find counter-evidence from your life. To complete this step, gather evidence that proves your belief is not true. For example, if you believe that you're just a "shy person," then look for times when you were confident rather than shy (e.g., when you are with your close friends and family).

_____

_____

_____

_____

_____

_____

_____

_____

3. Find counter-evidence from other people's lives. If you hold the belief, "It takes money to make money," find some counter-evidence from the lives of others. Maybe someone you know—a friend or a friend of a friend— was resourceful enough to start a business with very little capital and grow it into a large company. You could even read biographies and autobiographies of great people to serve as proof of empowering beliefs that can help battle those that limit you.

_____

_____

_____

_____

_____

_____

_____

4. Examine what the limiting beliefs are costing you. What opportunities are you missing out on? How is your life being limited by these beliefs? Ideally, this exercise will help bring to life the proof you need of how your limiting beliefs are impacting your life—motivating you to let go of these limiting beliefs.

_____

_____

_____

_____

_____

_____

_____

_____

5. Replace the old belief with a NEW belief that supports you. For example, instead of believing, "I am just a shy person," create a new belief that says, "I have been confident in the past, which means I'm capable of being confident. I can do so at will as long as I learn how."

_____

_____

_____

_____

_____

_____

_____

_____

6. Reinforce the new belief. **Whenever a disempowering belief shows up, use the "belief-opposition strategy."**Think of the new belief instead and consciously repeat it to yourself. It will force the old belief out. Keep reinforcing the new belief until it's your automatic response.

7. Take ACTION. Start making the new belief a reality. If your new belief is, "I believe I can become a confident person," take the first step that shows you can be a confident person. Go talk to someone, sign up to give that presentation at work, or do something that previously made you anxious/nervous. The more action you take in the direction of your belief, the more evidence you have for it, and the stronger it becomes! What action can you take today to make your new belief a reality? Write it down:

_____

_____

_____

_____

_____

_____

_____

_____

Once you've identified the beliefs you hold to be true, and you've followed the steps above to challenge and adjust those beliefs, you'll be even closer to your goal of learning to control your emotions.

IN A NUTSHELL

What Most People Do:

Non-resilient people:

- Hold beliefs that limit them
- Never consciously examine their beliefs
- Put difficult conditions on desired emotional states, which makes it difficult to experience the desired emotions

What Emotionally Resilient People Do Differently:

Resilient people:

- Consciously examine and mold their belief system
- Minimize conditions for desired emotional states so that they can experience those emotions more often
- Place difficult conditions on undesired emotional states to minimize those emotions
- Use the belief-opposition strategy to counter negative beliefs
- Create new beliefs that support their goals and desires
- Take immediate action to reinforce their new beliefs

Free Bonus:
My VIP Client Worksheet

Don't just read this book, take action! Grab a pen and paper and work through the questions and exercises highlighted in this book. Taking immediate action is the key to success. If you like, you can download the 1-page worksheet I use with my VIP clients to help them eliminate disempowering beliefs here:
www.AkashKaria.com/Bonus

"The difference in the quality of people's lives often comes down to the difference in the questions they consistently ask themselves."

~ Anthony Robbins

Chapter Five

THE HIDDEN POWER OF QUESTIONS

~

Habit 5:

Resilient people understand the power of questions

Your thoughts throughout the day are driven by questions that you ask yourself.

These questions drive your mental energy—whether you're aware of them or not.

The goal of this chapter is to help you identify the questions you ask and learn to understand how these questions guide your thinking (and therefore your emotions).

Let's take a look at a few questions that might sound familiar to you:

- "Why does my boss never respect me?"

- "Why is that person never on time?"

- "What did I do to deserve this?"

- "Why is life so unfair?"

Questions like these essentially set you up for negativity. **Even though these are loaded questions that contain untrue assumptions—or presuppositions—about yourself and other people, your brain will work to find an answer that fits regardless of whether it is true.**

Let's take a look at the first question as an example. When you ask yourself, "Why does my boss (or spouse/friend/etc.) never respect me?" the presupposition is that they *never* appreciate you! Your brain isn't going to challenge that presupposition unless it has been conditioned to do so. Moreover, because you've asked it a question, it will be compelled to come up with answers (even though they may not be accurate).

Here's another example: "Why am I such an idiot?" Obviously, the presupposition here is that you are, in fact, an idiot. Unfortunately, once you've asked yourself this question, your brain will come up with reasons to prove your idiocy.

Can you think of some of the negative, assumption-filled questions that *you* ask yourself on a daily basis? Are they leading you to unfair or untrue conclusions about yourself and others?

WOULD YOU LIKE TO MAKE A CHANGE?

Well, once you're aware of the questions you're asking and the assumptions they rely on, you can use them to your advantage. **When you find yourself asking a question that contains a presupposition, consciously challenge it**, and then ask questions that are more empowering and more likely to guide your life in the direction you desire.

For example, imagine that you're frustrated by your failure to meet a personal goal related to diet, weight, or exercise. It may feel natural to start asking questions like, "Why can I never achieve my goals?" or "Why am I so weak?" or "Why can I never make healthy choices?"

Rather than allowing your thoughts to head in such a disempowering direction, choose questions that contain more empowering presuppositions:

- "What can I learn from this?"

- "What goals in my life have I been successful in meeting? And how can I use those lessons to be successful at my new goals?"

Questions like these do a couple of things. First, they contain more positive presuppositions. For instance, the first question assumes that there is something to be learned from your experience. The second question assumes that you *have* had success meeting your goals in the past.

Questions like these also guide your mental energy in a more productive direction.

Rather than takingyou down a path of self-loathing, self-pity, and depression, questions like those in the previous paragraph encourage problem solving, positive thinking, and forward motion.

With the first question, you're learning from your mistakes and moving on. With the second question, you are focusing on past successes and hopefully working to identify a pattern—why were you able to be successful then, but not as much now? Has something changed?

You are the questions you ask yourself

SELF-AWARENESS IS PART OF SELF-MASTERY

By now, you're probably noticing a pattern of self-awareness. Much of your ability to control your emotions depends on your ability to be aware of all of the complex things going on inside your head. Suddenly, we're paying attention to the meaning we assign to events, we're aware of the things we tend to focus on, we're aware of the beliefs we hold, and now we're even aware of the questions we ask ourselves to drive our internal dialogue.

I know this sounds like a lot, but awareness is really half the battle. Once you're aware that all of these different processes are happening and that you have control over them, you're already well on your way to emotional resilience.

IN A NUTSHELL

What Most People Do:

Non-resilient people:

- Never pay attention to their thoughts and questions
- Never challenge questions with disempowering presuppositions
- Ask questions that put them into un-resourceful states

What Emotionally Resilient People Do Differently:

Resilient people:

- Understand the power of questions
- Challenge limiting, disempowering presuppositions
- Ask questions with empowering presuppositions that lead their life in more positive directions

"Did you know that every successful entrepreneur and executive has one thing that they share in common? They all have a strong and solid level of emotional resilience. Was it something that they were born with? No. For the most part they learned it as a skill that is absolutely essential to thrive in business."

~ Beverly Boston

Chapter Six

POWERFUL TRICKS FOR TAKING CONTROL OF YOUR MENTAL MOVIES

~

Habit 6:
Resilient people manage their self-talk and inner movies

When you think back on childhood memories, do certain smells, tastes, sounds, and pictures come to mind?

Some of those memories are probably pleasant ones—filled with the smiling faces of family members, the smell of dinner cooking on the stove, and the sound of laughter.

Some may be memories of events that are not as pleasant. For example, one of my friends shared this with me:

"I can remember riding my bike home from school one day with a few friends. There was a shortcut we liked to take down a gravel road with a fairly steep incline, and on this particular day, we were having a contest to see who could ride further without holding on to the handlebars. With our arms raised in the air, laughing and whooping triumphantly—I can still hear their voices and feel the wind in my hair—the inevitable happened.

"My front wheel hit a pothole, and I flew over the handlebars in slow motion. I've never forgotten the smell of the dirt under my head and the taste of gravel in my mouth. Needless to say, I didn't win the competition. I may not have been seriously injured, but my pride was; it's a memory that has stayed with me forever."

YOUR INTERNAL REPRESENTATIONS...

Do you have a memory that you can play back in your mind just as vividly? Complete with smells, tastes, sounds, feelings, and images? I'm sure you do, because that's how your brain works. As you experience external events, your brain interprets those events and puts together its own internal representation. **This representation becomes your reality and plays a large role in the way you react emotionally to the various events and memories you encounter.**

So how will knowing this help you on your road to emotional resilience?

Well, in order to achieve emotional resilience, it's important that you learn to take control of your internal representations—the things you see, hear, and feel inside your head.

"Great! Where do I start?" you may ask.

Before we start defining what this process *is*, let's start by defining what it *isn't*.

Changing your internal representations does not involve attempting to erase the past. Instead, we will be learning how to change the way we mentally represent events that happened in the past. By adjusting the way we remember events, we may be able to ultimately change the emotions associated with them.

HOW YOUR BRAIN RE-CREATES THE WORLD

Let's get started by learning a little more about how our brains process information.

When we experience an event, our brains create internal representations using primarily three of the five senses: visual (things you see), auditory (speech and other things you hear), and kinesthetic (things you feel physically and emotionally).

So when you find yourself in a negative emotional state (let's say, for example, "anger"), take a close look at what's going on inside your head. You'll soon realize a few things:

- You're seeing an image, picture, or movie in your head that makes you angry.

- You're saying certain things to yourself that make you angry ("How could she do this to me?!" or "How dare he treat me that way?"); you may even be hearing the other person saying certain things to you that make you angry. Chances are, you're probably repeating the hurtful words over and over.

- You may even be able to "feel" the other person's physical touch, or feel vibes or emotions they project like disrespect or arrogance. This is why people are sometimes able to say things like, "I just felt she hated me!" or "I just get a sense he doesn't like me."

Next, get ready for a fun change in career. You're going to be like a movie director, because you can literally change the movie playing inside your head by changing the visual, auditory, and kinesthetic aspects.

Time to direct your own movies

VISUAL – WHAT YOU SEE

So how can you change and control the visual representations in your mind? Let's practice. Think of something negative (but not *too* negative since this is your first attempt)—an experience you don't like. See it inside your head.

Once you have it, you'll find yourself instantly feeling negative emotions. Now close your eyes, pay close attention to the visual aspects of the memory you're recalling, and answer the following questions:

- Is the picture you see in **COLOR**? Or is it in black and white? Once you've determined that, switch it to the opposite setting. For example, if your memory is in full color, try changing it to black and white. Does this alteration change your emotions surrounding the event, or the meaning the event holds for you?

- Similarly, try adjusting the **BRIGHTNESS** of your memory by making it duller or by turning up the brightness. Does this change the way you feel at all?

- How much **SPACE** is between you and the picture? Is the action happening near you, or is it taking place far off in the distance? If the picture is off in the distance, try bringing it in closer, and if it's happening right in front of you, try pushing it further away. How do these changes impact how you feel about or interpret the event?

- How big is the picture? What happens when you manipulate the **SIZE** by making it either bigger or smaller?

- Next, let's see what happens when you manipulate your **ASSOCIATION** with the memory. First, view the scene as if you aren't in the picture at all. Instead, imagine that you are viewing the memory on a big screen at the cinema where you're sitting in the audience (disassociation). Next, view it with yourself in the scene, experiencing the event (association).

- What happens when you manipulate the **FOCUS** of your memory? Try taking it out of focus so that it is blurrier, and then bringing it into focus and making it as clear as you can. Do you notice any difference in how the memory makes you feel when it is blurry versus clearly focused?

Experiment with the above movie controls—brightness, color, focus, association, space, and size—and see what reduces and what increases the emotional intensity of the experience. For most people (though not for everyone— you'll have to try out the experiment on yourself to know for sure) **dissociating from an image, making it duller, removing the color from it, pushing it further away, and shrinking it in size dramatically removes the emotional hold of the event.**

Unfortunately, this is exactly what many people tend to do with the *positive* events in their life! Then for the negative events, they make them really big and up close with bright color, and they associate themselves within the event, giving the event an even more powerful hold over their emotions.

AUDITORY – WHAT YOU HEAR

In addition to manipulating the visual aspects of our memories, we can also change how we represent the auditory aspects. These are the things we are able to hear inside our heads—the things we say to ourselves, the things we can hear someone else saying to us or about us, etc.

When the things you're hearing are negative, wouldn't it be nice to have the power to change them and lessen their impact?

You do have that power! You just need to learn how it works. Ultimately, there are three auditory aspects that we can practice adjusting—just like we adjusted the pictures we saw above.

- First are the actual **WORDS** that we hear. Take a moment to think about the words you say to yourself when you're in a negative emotional state. What specific words do you use? For example, I know that when I used to lose my keys, I would say to myself, "I'm such an idiot! How could I lose my keys?" Then, I could even hear my ex-girlfriend berating me, saying, "That's so stupid! You're so careless!" (Yes, that is why she's my ex!)

    Those were the words I repeated to myself over and over—no wonder I was in such a negative state! So let's replace this with a more positive statement. Instead of, "I'm such an idiot for failing," for example, consciously change the words to, "I'm glad I made that mistake, because now I'll never make it again!"

By the way, it's okay to have a little fun with this. Sometimes, I just replace one or two words in the sentence to see the humorous impact it has. For instance, **instead of saying, "I'm such an idiot," I try, "I'm such a silly!" or "I'm such a cutie!" or even "I'm such a cutie McHottie!"** I know it sounds goofy, but it's effective and certainly helps lessen the depressing sideeffects of drowning in your own negative self-talk.

When trying to change *other* people's auditory representations in my head, I imaging giving them ridiculous pieces of dialogue. For example, rather than listen to my ex-girlfriend saying, **"You're so careless!" over and over in my mind, I mentally changed the dialogue to, "You're so careless, and I find that so sexy!"** Suddenly, that became very funny to me—it broke my negative emotional pattern!

- Next, try changing the **TONE** of the words you hear. This is an important step, because not only are the actual words themselves negative, but the tone they are spoken or heard in can be mean and condescending as well. Next time you're allowing your voice (or the voice of your ex, for example) to berate and belittle yourself, take control of the situation and change the tone.

Listening to the voice of Winnie the Pooh or some other famous character is sure to be far more entertaining than listening to your own (or those of others). I think you'll notice that this strategy is pretty effective in stopping negativity in its tracks—extra points if you get a laugh out of it, too!

In fact, maintaining a sense of humor in tough times is an important quality of emotionally resilient people. The research proves this:

"Looking at Holocaust victims, Maurice Vanderpol, a former president of the Boston Psychoanalytic Society and Institute, found that many of the healthy survivors of concentration camps had what he calls a "plastic shield." The shield was comprised of several factors, including a sense of humor. Often the humor was black, but nonetheless it provided a critical sense of perspective." – via Harvard Business Review

- The final auditory component you can practice manipulating is **VOLUME**. When you have a negative movie playing in your mind, is it really loud? Try hitting the imaginary mute button. The rude criticism coming from your coworker's mouth won't be nearly as damaging when you can't hear it! ("I'm sorry, what was that, Phillip? I can't seem to hear you—are you saying that you appreciate the three days I spent putting together this presentation? Thanks!")

You can use this same principle with positive memories, but you'll want to turn them up instead of down. Practice really does make perfect with this one. Before you know it, you'll be a master of mental volume control.

KINESTHETIC – WHAT YOU FEEL

Next, let's talk about the kinesthetic aspects of our memories and thoughts; remember, this could be a memory that makes you feel something physically *or* emotionally. Just as we did above, we're going to practice making changes to a couple of the kinesthetic aspects of our memories.

- First, try adjusting the **INTENSITY** of the negative memory you're recalling. How intense is the sensation it makes you feel? Now, imagine you had a magical dial that could reduce the strength of the feeling, and turn it down. Then, turn it down a little further, and see if that changes how you feel. (As silly as this sounds, it actually works!)

- Does your memory come with a sensation of weight or **PRESSURE**? What happens if you imagine attaching a balloon to the weight, and feeling the pressure decrease? Does that help to reduce some of the intensity and relieve any pressure the memory causes?

- Finally, try to pinpoint the **LOCATION** of any sensation you're feeling. From where does it seem to be originating? What if you move it to another location, or move it out of your body completely? For example, if you're feeling butterflies in your stomach, imagine watching them leave your body and flutter away.

While playing around with the different controls of the visual, auditory, and kinesthetic aspects of your memories might seem like a strange thing to do (I know it did for me at first), it's a very powerful exercise. **It scrambles your internal representations and breaks the negative emotional pattern—allowing you more control over your emotional state.**

IN A NUTSHELL

What Most People Do:

Non-resilient people:

- Relive negative experiences over and over again in their head

What Emotionally Resilient People Do Differently:

Resilient people:

- Take control of their self-talk and inner-movies
- Break the hold of negative events by scrambling their internal representations
- Amplify desired emotions using visual, auditory, and kinesthetic controls

"More than education, more than experience, more than training, a person's level of resilience will determine who succeeds and who fails. That's true in the cancer ward, it's true in the Olympics, and it's true in the boardroom."

~ Dean Becker
via Harvard Business Review

Chapter Seven

THE ABC LOOP
~

Habit 7:
Resilient people use future pacing to control the ABC loop

When I was in high school, I had a very high temper, and it wasn't easy for me to control it. For example, in eleventh grade, I wound up getting into a physical fight at least once a week; by the time I graduated, I had physically fought half the boys in the grade above me and at least half of those in the grade below.

So what was my trigger?

Any time someone said anything about me—be it criticizing, making fun of something I did or said, or laughing at me (or behind my back)—I immediately felt embarrassment due to my low self-esteem at the time. The embarrassment would quickly turn to anger, and I would begin to feel a rising pressure inside myself. I felt myself beginning to tense up, my eyes would narrow, my hands would automatically curl into fists, and I'd lunge at the guy who had embarrassed me in the first place—entirely prepared to pummel him into the ground.

Now my fighting days are over, and they're not something I'm proud of; as you can see, anger was a serious issue for me.

But what about now?

Now, I am one of the calmest people I now; it takes a lot to make me angry. If you were to ask my friends or anyone who knows me to describe me, they would almost certainly use words like "calm," "rational," and "level-headed." This doesn't mean that I never get upset, but it does mean that I no longer allow my anger to control me. While anger has its place and can be very effective (and even appropriate in certain circumstances), I've found that there are better ways of meeting my needs and achieving the outcomes I desire.

So what made the difference for me?

I was reading a book by Dr. Ben Carson titled *Gifted Hands* that gives a first-hand account of Carson's evolution from a troubled inner city youth to a world-renowned pediatric neurosurgeon. In one particular part of the book that really spoke to me, he described how his own anger problems nearly led him to kill someone:

"I had real anger issues. I would just fly off the handle and really become quite irrational and try to hurt people with baseball bats, hammers, whatever. In this particular case, I happened to have a large camping knife. And, you know, one of my friends angered me. And I just lunged at his abdomen with the knife. Probably would have seriously injured or killed him, but he happened to have on a large metal belt buckle under his clothing, upon which the blade broke.

And, of course, he fled in terror. But I was more horrified than he was, because I realized that I was trying to kill somebody over nothing — and that I would never realize my dreams of becoming a physician. And I would end up in jail, reform school, or the grave. And I just locked myself in the bathroom and started praying…"

When I read that, I instantly connected with the situation because that's exactly what I had felt like; while I hadn't yet tried to kill someone, I knew that if I let my anger get the best of me, the possibility probably wasn't too far out of bounds.

Do you have a certain pattern of behavior of which you wish you could rid yourself? If it isn't anger, maybe it's jealousy, laziness, being judgmental or critical of others, overeating, or something different.

Regardless of what it is, it's not too late to change!

Before I explain how I was able to kick my struggle with anger and aggression to the curb, let's take a look at something called the sequencing of emotional habits.

Whenever we have an emotional habit, it follows the following ABC sequence:

- A = Antecedent (the stimulus)

- B = Behavior

- C = Consequence

Let's take a quick look at examples from my life to help define each of these elements:

- Antecedent (stimulus) = A boy in class makes fun of the size of my nose, which triggers the emotion of embarrassment, followed by anger. The pressure builds.

- Behavior = The emotions I feel lead me to lunge toward the boy with my fists balled up.

- Consequence = Anger disappears, and the pressure is released. I have some bruises and receive punishment from the teachers.

Now, let's take a look at the ABC sequence for an emotional response that *you* regularly experience. Once you have it in mind, think about the kinds of things that act as your trigger. These things would be antecedents, or stimuli.

Are you able to change the antecedent?

For instance, if you find yourself being tempted to eat chocolate while you're on your diet, then why not toss it out of the house? By getting rid of the antecedent, you negate or change the emotional response as well as the succeeding behavior and consequence. (This is why I avoid keeping any kind of junk food in my house.)

Want to lose weight? Toss out the junk food!

What is the behavior that results from the antecedent and emotional response? When I found myself becoming angry, there was a typical sequence of events, beginning with the balling of my fists. If I'd simply changed my behavior—in this case, my physiology—by relaxing my hands and loosening the tension in my muscles, I may have managed to trigger a different, more relaxed and productive emotional state.

So how can you change your behavior, beginning with the first in the sequence, in order to change the emotion? **Emotion leads to behavior, but as we've discussed, behavior also leads to emotion.**

Now consider the consequences of your behavior—what reward or punishment do you receive as a result of the behavior? This is so important to really think about and understand. If I had taken just a brief second to think about the consequences of fighting (bruises, unpopularity in class, and detentions from the teacher), my anger probably would have been lessened, as I definitely did not want to experience these consequences.

So take a moment to really think: what consequences do your emotional habits result in?

FUTURE PACING

Now that we've talked about the ABC sequence and the negative impact our emotional responses to stimuli often have, let's talk about how to make a change. The technique I ultimately started using is called "futurepacing," although I wasn't aware that was what it was called at the time.

Here's how it works:

First, you imagine a future situation in which you encounter the antecedent(the stimulus). For me, this would have been somebody making fun of me for something like the size of my nose (I have a big nose, but I've come to accept myself and love myself for who I am) or something I said. For you, maybe it's a coworker saying something rude, the sound of your children bickering with each other, or a messy, disorganized house.

Now, instead of immediately jumping right to the automatic behavior (anger-fueled fist fighting for me), **visualize yourself having the ability to consciously choose the emotion you feel.** Whereas you previously used to get angry, you now imagine yourself handling the same stimulus with a sense of calm.

Then, imagine yourself performing a different, more productive behavior (e.g., taking in some deep breaths to calm yourself down, walking away from the situation, etc.) and as a result, having a more desirable consequence (e.g., feeling better about yourself, friends supporting you for behaving in a more mature manner, etc.).

By futurepacing (stepping into the future and visualizing a new ABC pattern), I was ultimately able to create the neural pathways in my brain that allowed me to perform a new, more productive pattern when encountering the offending antecedent. Research has actually shown that simply visualizing something creates neural pathways in your brain. Angie LeVan, a resilience coach who has worked with the United States Army, writes in *Psychology Today*:

> "A study looking at brain patterns in weightlifters found that the patterns activated when a weightlifter lifted hundreds of pounds were similarly activated when they only imagined lifting. **In some cases, research has revealed that mental practices are almost effective as true physical practice, and that doing both is more effective than either alone.** For instance, in his study on everyday people, Guang Yue, an exercise psychologist from Cleveland Clinic Foundation in Ohio, compared "people who went to the gym with people who carried out virtual workouts in their heads". He found that a 30% muscle increase in the group who went to the gym. However, the group of participants who conducted mental exercises of the weight training increased muscle strength by almost half as much (13.5%)."

For example, if you visualize picking up a basketball, bouncing it a couple of times, and shooting it straight through the hoop, your brain goes through the same process it would if you were actually physically bouncing and shooting a basketball. This helps you learn to do something or become familiar with an action or situation before you encounter it in reality.

Many successful and emotionally resilient people believe and practice visualization. Matt Mayberry, a fellow speaker and maximum performance strategist, writes in his column in *Entrepreneur:*

- "Boxing legend Muhammad Ali was always stressing the importance of seeing himself victorious long before the actual fight.

- As a struggling young actor, Jim Carrey used to picture himself being the greatest actor in the world.

- Michael Jordan always took the last shot in his mind before he ever took one in real life."

So give it a try! I'll walk you through it. Start by visualizing the antecedent that typically triggers your undesirable emotional response. Once you've identified a specific trigger, futurepace by imagining yourself encountering this same stimulus at some time in the future, only this time (using the tools you've learned in this book), you choose a new emotional response. See yourself performing the new behavior and therefore enjoying a better consequence.

Remember, this wasn't just a one-time exercise—practice futurepacing on a regular basis to help you brain become more familiar with the emotional and behavioral response you wish to have under certain circumstances. Then, when those circumstances arise, you will be far more likely to succeed.

So that's the final tool of emotionally resilient people: they stay strong by futurepacing. While you can't realistically prepare for *every* situation you might encounter, there are certain habitual emotional patterns you're immersed in. For those, you can futurepace and create a new ABC loop.

IN A NUTSHELL

What Most People Do:

Non-resilient people:

- Get caught up in negative ABC loops

What Emotionally Resilient People Do Differently:

Resilient people:

- Understand the power of ABC loops
- Change the antecedent to break free of a negative ABC loop
- Use future pacing to lessen the hold of un-resourceful emotional patterns

Free Bonus:
13-Day Companion Guide

Congratulations for having made it this far into the book. We're almost at the end! But if you want more, then I have a companion 13-day inspirational guide that I'm currently offering for free. Over 17,000 people have downloaded the guide at:
www.AkashKaria.com/Bonus

"Who doesn't get derailed by the small setbacks of the everyday—flight getting cancelled, childcare plans falling apart, computer problems foiling the meeting? Resilience gives people the strength to overcome obstacles and bounce back."

~ Jan Bruce
via *Forbes*

Chapter Eight

WRAP UP

Your emotional habits—the ones we've explored in this book—determine the quality of your life and your business.

Thus, rather than living on autopilot and allowing your emotional responses to define your behavior and your life, climb back into the driver's seat and put some of these strategies and habits to the test—you won't be disappointed.

Just a quick review and to bring everything back full circle, here's a list of the seven things emotionally resilient people do differently:

1) They acknowledge their emotions, accept responsibility for them, and learn to interpret the positive intentions of their emotions.

2) They master their emotions through their physiology.

3) They consciously control the meaning of events through their focus.

4) They mold their belief system.

5) They understand the power of questions.

6) They manage their self-talk and inner movies.

7) They use futurepacing to control the ABC loop.

From my years as a coach and student of human behavior, I've found that these habits are the seven mostimportant habits for developing emotional resilience. **Using them, you'll be able to successfully navigate the vulnerabilities of relationships, the risks and failures of business, and the ups and downs of life.** In other words, you'll be able to use your emotions to achieve more success in life and business.

ONE MORE THING

This is the end of the book, but it doesn't have to be the end of our relationship. In fact, there is one *very* special gift that I've been holding off till the end.

As a thank-you for reading this book, I'd like to offer you for free my 60-minute audiobook, *How Successful People Think Differently*.

The book currently has 65 positive reviews on Amazon and if you like, you can purchase it here: http://viewbook.at/Success

Alternatively, you can get the audio version of the book for FREE. It's my way of over-delivering on the promise of this book by giving you extra tools and resources to help you on your success journey. You can grab the audiobook here: www.AkashKaria.com/Bonus. (And remember, to unlock the emotional resilience quiz, use the access code: 7263). Please keep this link private, thank you. ☺

FINAL WORDS

I hope you've found value in this book. Use it as your reference and guide; re-read chapters and make notes as you work to put each strategy into practice.

Most importantly, be kind, patient and honest with yourself throughout this learning process. Allow yourself to see and accept your emotional responses as they are. This will ultimately make it easier to create change and reshape the way you react to every-day stimuli.

To developing your emotional resilience,

Akash Karia

ABOUT THE AUTHOR

Akash Karia is a resilience and peak performance coach who has trained over 80,000 people worldwide, from bankers in Hong Kong to senior executives in Switzerland to government members in Dubai.

Here's what experts and Akash's clients say about him:

"Akash is a wonderful professional speaker who has a great message, is motivating, inspiring and interactive at the same time...!"
~ Brian Tracy, Hall of Fame Speaker & #1 Bestselling Author of *Maximum Achievement*

"Akash is a phenomenal coach! The information I gained in just a few short hours is priceless."
~Fatema Dewji, Director of Marketing for a billion-dollar conglomerate

"Akash is THE best coach I've ever had!"
~ Eric Laughton, Certified John Maxwell Trainer

"Akash Karia is a rare talent who has much in store for you as an individual, and better yet, your organization."
~ Sherilyn Pang, Business Reporter, Capital TV, Malaysia

"The two days in Akash's workshop have been excellent, very informative and packed with knowledge...tons of practical, ready to use techniques."
~ Edyte Peszlo, Sales and Procurement Manager, Thailand

"This is the third time I've attended Akash's session...and once again, I'm mesmerized. Akash is a charismatic and effective speaker, coach and trainer! I look forward to his next session in Dubai!"
~ Vida Mamaril, Dubai, KHDA, Government of Dubai

"Akash delivered true value to our global sales team...relevant insights and tools that we can immediately implement in the market!"
~ Mark Butterman, InFront Sports, Switzerland

Subject to availability, Akash conducts keynotes, workshops and seminars internationally on the topics such as employee engagement, emotional resilience and peak performance psychology. Get in touch with him on **www.AkashKaria.com/Speaking**. Alternatively, you can email him on Akash@AkashKaria.com or akash.speaker@gmail.com.

CONNECT WITH AKASH

Grab your Free Success Toolkit:
www.AkashKaria.com/Bonus

Check out more Great books:
http://viewauthor.at/Akash

Email for Speaking/TrainingInquires:
akash@akashkaria.com / akash.speaker@gmail.com

Connect on LinkedIn:
www.LinkedIn.com/In/AkashKaria

Connect on Twitter:
@Speaking_Coach

You Might Also Enjoy

If you enjoyed this book, then you'll love this:

READY, SET...PROCRASTINATE! 23 ANTI-PROCRASTINATION TOOLS DESIGNED TO HELP YOU STOP PUTTING THINGS OFF AND START GETTING THINGS DONE

"This is one book you should not delay reading!

Having struggled with procrastination for much of my life, Akash Karia's book came like a breath of fresh air. He provides clear, practical advice on how to overcome the

problem, but warns that you will need to work at it daily. This is a quick, very useful read and with 23 tips on offer, there will be several that you can identify with and implement for immediate results. If there is just one thing that you should not put off, it is reading this book."
~ Gillian Findlay

"This is **a great manual on how to improve your everyday productivity**: stopping procrastination will mean you get the best from your activities and feel satisfied with everything you accomplish. The book gives very useful tips [that are] easy to follow and effective in their application."
~ Rosalinda Scalia

Grab the book here:
http://viewbook.at/procrastination

Made in the USA
San Bernardino, CA
01 March 2018